Concert and Contest COLLECTION

Compiled and Edited by H. VOXMAN

for

OBOE with piano accompaniment

▶ **Solo Oboe**

CONTENTS

RUBANK ®

HAL·LEONARD CORPORATION
7777 W. BLUEMOUND RD. P.O. BOX 13819 MILWAUKEE, WI 53213

Ariette
from Panurge

Oboe

A. E. M. GRÉTRY
Transcribed by H. Voxman

Aria and Rondinella

Oboe

G. F. HANDEL
Transcribed by H. Voxman

Two Menuettos
from Flute Sonata in C

Oboe

I

J. S. BACH
Transcribed by H. Voxman

II

Gavotta

Oboe

A. GOEDICKE, Op. 80, No. 1
Transcribed by H. Voxman

[poco rit.]
D. C. al Fine

Menuetto and Presto
from Trio V

Oboe

F. J. HAYDN
Transcribed by H. Voxman

Romance

Oboe

R. SCHUMANN, Op. 94, No. 1
Edited by H. Voxman

Sinfonia
(Arioso)
from Cantata No. 156*

Oboe

J. S. BACH
Transcribed by H. Voxman

* This Cantata was composed by Bach ca. 1730. The original scoring of the Sinfonia is for solo oboe, strings, and continuo. The eighth-note accompaniment figures (treble) should probably be played quasi pizzicato. Bach also used this melody in a more elaborate version in his F minor Concerto for clavier.

Mélodie

Oboe

CLÉMENT LENOM
Edited by H. Voxman

Andante and Allegro
from Sonata in G Major

Oboe

Edited by H. Voxman

J. B. LOEILLET
Arr. by A. Béon

Pièce in G Minor

Oboe

GABRIEL PIERNÉ, Op. 5
Edited by H. Voxman

Adagio and Allegro

Oboe

LEROY OSTRANSKY

Poco meno mosso

Tempo I

Sonata No. 1

Oboe

G. F. HANDEL
Edited by H. Voxman

* Begin all trills in the Sonata on the upper note.

Oboe

Sonatina
Based on Divertimento No. 2

Oboe

W. A. MOZART
Transcribed by H. Voxman

Oboe

TRIO

Menuetto da capo al Fine

Allegro Moderato
from Trio No. 1 (London)

Oboe

F. J. HAYDN
Adapted by R. Hervig

Colloquy

Oboe

IRA P. SCHWARZ